THE HISTORY OF TOYS

HELEN COX CANNONS

raintree

Raintree is an imprint of Capstone Global Library Limited, a company incorporated in England and Wales having its registered office at 264 Banbury Road, Oxford, OX2 7DY – Registered company number: 6695582

www.raintree.co.uk
myorders@raintree.co.uk

Text © Capstone Global Library Limited 2020
The moral rights of the proprietor have been asserted.

All rights reserved. No part of this publication may be reproduced in any form or by any means (including photocopying or storing it in any medium by electronic means and whether or not transiently or incidentally to some other use of this publication) without the written permission of the copyright owner, except in accordance with the provisions of the Copyright, Designs and Patents Act 1988 or under the terms of a licence issued by the Copyright Licensing Agency, Barnard's Inn, 86 Fetter Lane, London, EC4A 1EN (www.cla.co.uk). Applications for the copyright owner's written permission should be addressed to the publisher.

Editor: Clare Lewis
Designer: Justin Hoffmann – Pixelfox.co.uk
Media researcher: Tracy Cummins
Original illustrations © Capstone Global Library Limited 2020
Production Specialist: Laura Manthe
Originated by Capstone Global Library Ltd
Printed and bound in India

ISBN 978 1 4747 9260 8 (hardback)
ISBN 978 1 4747 9262 2 (paperback)

British Library Cataloguing in Publication Data
A full catalogue record for this book is available from the British Library.

Acknowledgements
We would like to thank the following for permission to reproduce photographs: Alamy: INTERFOTO, 20, My Childhood Memories, 18 top; iStockphoto: BrendanHunter, 17, CatLane, 24, CTRPhotos, 21, fieldwork, 12 right, fotoVoyager, 5 right, ivanastar, 15, JazzIRT, 12–13; Shutterstock: Billion Photos, cover middle left, charles taylor, 19, dcwcreations, 14, dnd_project, 23, ESOlex, 18 bottom, ExVoto78, 16, Gyvafoto, 6 right, Haver, cover middle right, Ivan_Sabo, 25 bottom, JakeOwenPowell, 12 left, Jason Dudley, 22, Jennie Book, 28, LiliGraphie, 4, Makistock, 29, mervas, 27 bottom, OksanaAriskinas, cover left, back cover, padu_foto, 25 top, robtek, 26, SamJonah, 10, 11, Stelian-Radu Borlovan, 27 top, Steve Mann, 13, studio BM, cover right, Vaide Seskauskiene, 6 left, Zarya Maxim Alexandrovich, 5 left; SuperStock: ClassicStock.com, 8, 9, J.Bauer/Mauritius, 7

Every effort has been made to contact copyright holders of material reproduced in this book. Any omissions will be rectified in subsequent printings if notice is given to the publisher.

All the internet addresses (URLs) given in this book were valid at the time of going to press. However, due to the dynamic nature of the internet, some addresses may have changed, or sites may have changed or ceased to exist since publication. While the author and publisher regret any inconvenience this may cause readers, no responsibility for any such changes can be accepted by either the author or the publisher.

London Borough of Enfield	
91200000706058	
Askews & Holts	13-Nov-2020
J688.7209 JUNIOR NON	
ENOAKW	

Contents

Past and present 4
The 1900s and 1910s: simple games and toys.................. 6
The 1920s: toy trains and pedal cars 8
The 1930s and 1940s: board games 10
The 1950s: toy cars, Play-doh and Barbie 12
The 1960s: Lego, spaceships and robots 16
The 1970s: Star Wars and Pong 20
The 1980s: the Rubik's Cube and Sega Mega Drive 22
The 1990s: talking pets and computer games 24
The 2000s to today: eSports and loom bands 26
What has changed over the years?.................................. 28
Glossary 30
Find out more 31
Index 32

Some words are shown in bold, **like this**. You can find out what they mean by looking in the glossary.

Past and present

Did you know that children played with toys thousands of years ago? Children in ancient Rome played with yo-yos, marbles and skipping ropes. Children in ancient China played with puppets, kites and dolls. In ancient India, children played board games like Snakes and Ladders.

Then and Now

Many toys from ancient times, such as yo-yos, marbles and dolls, are still played with now.

This photograph shows a boy with his Christmas presents. It was taken in the early 1900s.

| 1900s | 1910s | 1920s | 1930s | 1940s | 1950s |

Looking at toys can tell you a lot about the time they were made. Toy cars that were made in the early 1900s looked very different from today's toy cars. Many toys used to be made of metal and wood. Today they are often made of plastic.

old toy car

These are modern toys. Have you played with toys like these?

FACT

The first plastic toys were made in the 1940s. A toy company called Fisher Price was the first to make them.

| 1960s | 1970s | 1980s | 1990s | 2000s | 2010s |

The 1900s and 1910s: simple games and toys

In the 1900s, children often made their own toys. Children would make dolls out of rags and wooden pegs. They used sticks for swords or made **catapults** from sticks and elastic. Many children's games were played outdoors, such as tag, hopscotch and hide and seek.

Popular toys from toy shops included dolls, **clockwork** toys, spinning tops, puzzles, rocking horses and toy soldiers.

spinning top

Lots of children liked to play with tin toy soldiers, like these. This is because many of their fathers were soldiers in **World War I**.

A construction toy called Meccano was first made in the 1900s. It quickly became very popular. Children could build cars made of strips of metal fixed together using nuts and bolts. You could even bolt on wheels.

Then and Now

One hundred years ago, children did not have as many toys as they do now.

Stuffed bears were also popular. The first bear with moving arms and legs was **invented** in Germany in 1902. In the same year, an American man created another stuffed bear. He called it "Teddy's Bear".

FACT

"Teddy's Bear" was named after Theodore "Teddy" Roosevelt. Roosevelt was an American president. That is how the teddy bear got its name.

The 1920s: toy trains and pedal cars

In the 1920s, trains, cars, boats and aeroplanes were all becoming faster. Tickets were cheaper to buy than before. More people were able to travel. Model cars, trains, boats and aeroplanes became popular toys.

Before the 1920s, toy trains were either push-along ones or **clockwork** ones that children wound up and let go. In 1925, a toy maker called Frank Hornby sold an **electric** train set.

Toy trains were made to look just like trains of the time.

Pedal cars looked like **miniature** versions of real cars. They became very popular. Children would make them go by pushing on pedals, like on a bicycle.

Children mostly played with toys based on their **gender**. Boys were given chemistry sets, building sets and electric toys. Girls played with sewing kits, dolls, tea sets and toy cookers.

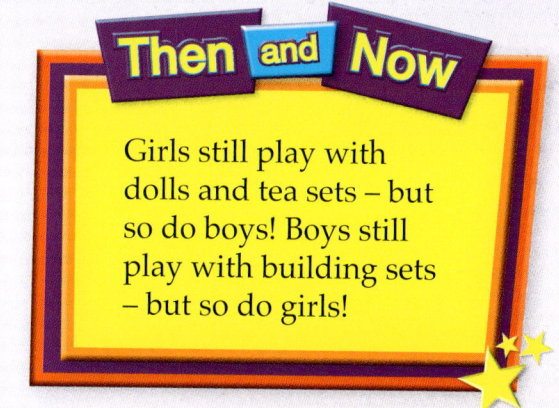

Then and Now

Girls still play with dolls and tea sets – but so do boys! Boys still play with building sets – but so do girls!

Pedal cars were expensive to buy so they were mainly owned by rich families.

The 1930s and 1940s: board games

In the 1930s many people lost their jobs and many families were very poor. People could not afford to buy a lot of toys. Children played with old toys.

Then and Now

Toys used to have sharp edges or loose parts. Now toy makers have to make sure toys are safe for babies and children.

However, people still liked playing games about money. The board game Monopoly became popular. It is about buying houses and hotels and getting rich.

This is an old version of Monopoly.

From 1939 to 1945, Britain was at war again. Children's toys were in short supply. Many toy factories were needed to make **weapons** or machines.

Some toy factories kept making toys, but they were made more simply or cheaply. Teddy bears had less **stuffing** in them. Meccano's usual green and red parts were plain metal because there was not enough paint.

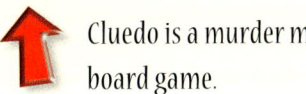
Cluedo is a murder mystery board game.

After the war ended, toy factories opened up again. Board games such as Cluedo and Scrabble were first made in the 1940s.

Many families still like to play board games together. But now people can also play computer and video games with their families.

| 1960s | 1970s | 1980s | 1990s | 2000s | 2010s |

The 1950s: toy cars, Play-doh and Barbie

After World War II ended, more babies were born. This was known as the "Baby Boom". Because of this, there was also a boom in the toy industry. Toy makers started to use plastic. Plastic toys could be produced in greater numbers and more cheaply. Popular plastic toys included Mr Potato Head, frisbees, hula-hoops and Etch-a-sketch.

Then and Now

Mr Potato Head, frisbees, hula-hoops and Etch-a-sketch are all toys that are still played with. Do you have any of these toys?

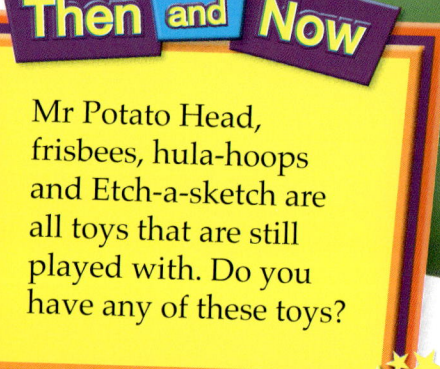

Mr Potato Head

An original Etch-a-sketch

frisbee

One of the top-selling toys of the 1950s was the toy car. Two famous companies, Matchbox and Corgi, made small model cars. Matchbox cars were given that name because they could fit in a matchbox.

Corgi cars had plastic windows, boots and **bonnets** that opened. There were also toy lorries, fire engines, buses, delivery vans and more. They were light, easy to carry and didn't cost much to buy.

This matchbox toy is advertising the cereal Weetabix.

| 1960s | 1970s | 1980s | 1990s | 2000s | 2010s |

Play-doh started out as wallpaper cleaner! It was made of salt, water and flour. In 1949, the company started selling it as a craft and play **material**. In 1956 it was named Play-Doh.

Play-Doh is soft and can be made into shapes and models. It has become one of the most popular toys ever.

FACT

More than 3 billion pots of Play-Doh have been sold. That's enough to reach the Moon and back three times!

| 1900s | 1910s | 1920s | 1930s | 1940s | **1950s** |

The Barbie doll was created in 1959 by Ruth Handler. In 1961, Handler made the Ken doll. Both Barbie and Ken were named after Handler's own children. About 58 million Barbie dolls are still sold every year. Barbie and Ken's faces, clothes and hair have changed a lot since the 1950s.

Ken

Barbie

FACT

Barbie Fact File
Full name: Barbara "Barbie" Millicent Roberts
Born: 9 March 1959
From: Willows, Wisconsin, USA
First outfit: a black-and-white swimsuit
Best friend: Kenneth "Ken" Sean Carson
Best-selling Barbie: The 1992 Totally Hair™ Barbie with floor-length hair
Favourite colour: pink

| 1960s | 1970s | 1980s | 1990s | 2000s | 2010s |

The 1960s: Lego, spaceships and robots

In the 1960s, games such as Twister and Operation were first played. Toy makers were also making toys **electric** as much as they could.

Toys began to have flashing lights, moving parts or electronic voices. If a toy was electric it was thought of as new and exciting.

Then and Now

Electric toys using batteries were quite new in the 1960s. Now there are thousands of toys and games that need batteries.

These police car toys from the 1960s were electric.

The original Thunderbird 4 toy

Toys and games were made using popular TV and film characters of the day. These included Batman, Winnie the Pooh, Dennis the Menace and Thunderbirds.

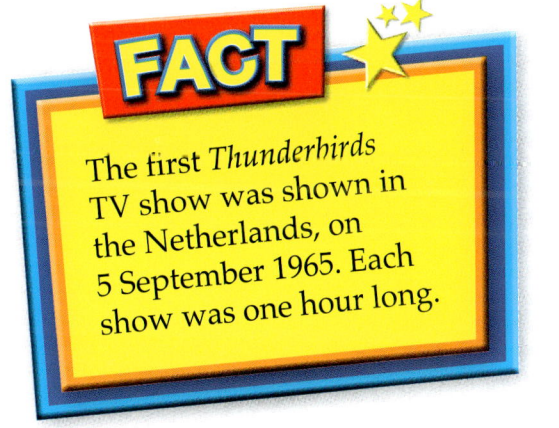

FACT

The first *Thunderbirds* TV show was shown in the Netherlands, on 5 September 1965. Each show was one hour long.

1960s 1970s 1980s 1990s 2000s 2010s

The Toy of the Year Awards were launched in 1965. The first winner was the Aston Martin toy car from the James Bond films. Other winners in the 1960s were Action Man, Spirograph and Hot Wheels cars.

Aston Martin

One of the most popular toys of the 1960s was Lego. The Lego company was started by a Danish man called Ole Kirk Christiansen. Lego bricks were wooden until the late 1960s. Then they became plastic, as they are now.

Lego is short for the two Danish words "leg godt", which means "play well".

In 1961, Russian **cosmonaut** Yuri Gagarin became the first man in space. Then, on 20 July 1969, American **astronauts** Neil Armstrong and Buzz Aldrin became the first people to walk on the Moon.

The huge interest in space travel during the 1960s led to lots of space toys being made. These included robots and spaceships.

Then and Now

Robot and spaceship toys now have a lot more buttons on them and often make noises. **Electric** space toys in the 1960s were much simpler.

1960s | 1970s | 1980s | 1990s | 2000s | 2010s

The 1970s: Star Wars and Pong

Improvements in **technology** in the 1970s meant that more and more toys were electronic. In the 1970s the first handheld computer games were made. One of these was Simon. It was named after the game "Simon Says…".

Simon's buttons lit up and the player had to copy the pattern. The game is still sold today.

Then and Now

Many years ago, dolls did not "do" anything. Now they can cry, be fed and can "wee" or "poo". Dolls now often have batteries so they can talk and move.

Another popular toy made in the 1970s was the Baby Alive Doll. It could be fed and given a bottle and it "pooped". This kind of doll was new and very exciting.

The first video games were also created in the 1970s. In 1972 the American company Atari released Pong. Pong was a home video version of ping-pong. It quickly became very popular. More and more people had video games in their homes.

Like in the 1960s, many toys of the 1970s were based on children's TV show or films. These included *Doctor Who*, *Superman* and – the most popular of all – *Star Wars*. *Star Wars* action figures and toys were played with all over the world.

This Millennium Falcon toy was made in 1979.

The 1980s: the Rubik's Cube and Sega Mega Drive

By the 1980s, toy companies were making more and more computer games. The Japanese company Nintendo created Game and Watch **handheld devices**. Each one had a game and was also an alarm clock. Game characters included Donkey Kong and Mario Bros.

Then and Now

Children in the early 1900s did not have computer games. They had not yet been **invented**.

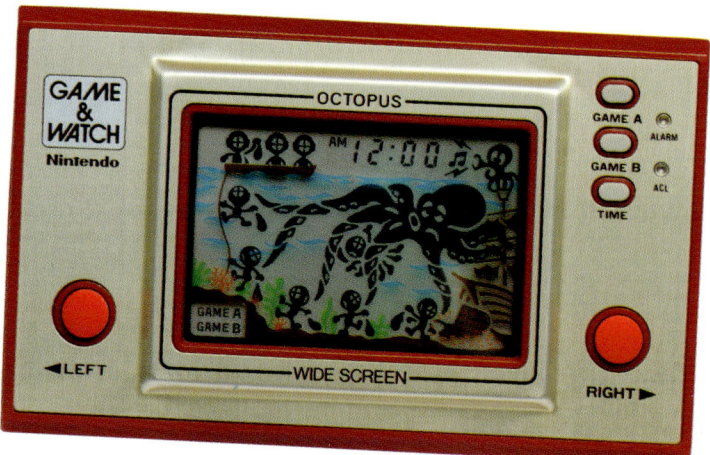

The Game and Watch Octopus game

In 1988, the company Sega made a video game **console** called the Sega Genesis – known as the Sega Mega Drive. All these video games were hugely popular.

The Rubik's Cube was winner of the Toy of the Year award in 1980 and 1981. The Rubik's Cube is a cube with different coloured squares on it. The aim is to move the squares round to get the same coloured squares on each side of the cube.

FACT

The world record for solving an original-shaped Rubik's cube is 3.47 seconds! This was done in 2018 by Yusheng Du of China.

Rubik's Cube

Collectable dolls and toys were very popular during the 1980s. There were cuddly toys, such as Cabbage Patch Kids. They had a plastic head, cloth body and woolly hair. My Little Pony and Sylvanian Families were collectable plastic animal characters.

The 1990s: talking pets and computer games

In the 1990s there was a **craze** for electronic toys that children could "care" for. These included Furbys and Tamagotchis. The Furby spoke its own language of "Furbish". The Tamagotchi was a handheld "digital pet" on a keyring. Children pressed buttons to feed or play with the pet on the screen. If they did not feed it, it would "die".

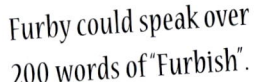

Furby could speak over 200 words of "Furbish".

Then and Now

In the early 1900s, toys were mostly sold in only a few countries. Now, toys such as computer games can be sold all over the world. This is because toys can be delivered more easily and quickly to different countries.

Computer games became more exciting to play. The Nintendo Game Boy was made in 1991. Pokémon was one of the first Game Boy characters. Sony PlayStation was made in 1994. The Sega Mega Drive made the first Sonic the Hedgehog game. Millions of these games were bought around the world.

The original Game Boy

Leonardo

The Teenage Mutant Ninja Turtles action figures were popular in the 1990s. There were four ninja turtles, all named after famous Italian artists: Leonardo, Michelangelo, Donatello and Raphael.

1960s | 1970s | 1980s | **1990s** | 2000s | 2010s

The 2000s to today: eSports and loom bands

Games **consoles** such as Nintendo Wii, Nintendo DS, Xbox 360 and PlayStation 3 were all made in the 2000s. The Nintendo Wii was so popular in Britain that it sold out! Minecraft was first made in 2011. It is one of the world's most popular games.

Then and Now

Video games now have lots of features. Old games made for the Sega Mega Drive were much simpler.

Some video games are now played as eSports. An eSport is when people compete to win a video game. Fortnite was made in 2017. It is one of the most popular ever video games. More than 250 million players play worldwide.

Mario Kart was one of the first Nintendo Wii games.

Toys of the 2000s were Littlest Pet Shop toys and Go Go Pet Hamsters. The Disney film *Frozen* came out in 2014. The Frozen Snow Glow Elsa Doll was a popular Christmas present that year.

Littlest Pet Shop toy

Rainbow Loom bands were a **craze**. They are tiny elastic bands in lots of different colours. They could be joined together to make bracelets, necklaces and charms.

Rainbow Loom bands were popular with children all over the world.

What has changed over the years?

Many toys that children played with in the early 1900s are still played with today. Children still enjoy train sets, toy cars, dolls and teddy bears. Board games that were created a long time ago have hardly changed.

FACT

Video and computer games make up nearly half of all toys and games that are sold.

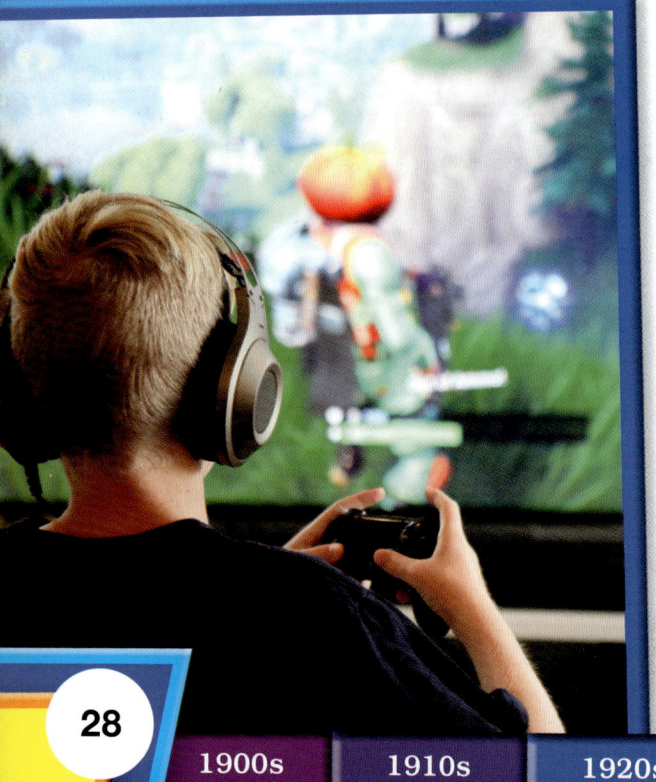

Children now have many more toys than children did 100 years ago. Children used to play outside a lot. Now children are more often indoors playing with toys or games.

A child from the 1900s would be amazed by games such as Fortnite! Televisions and computers as we know them today had not been **invented** then.

Toys used to be made of wood and metal. Now, most toys are made of plastic. We now know that plastic is bad for the **environment**. Parts of toys can get into rivers and seas. They can harm animals such as fish, turtles, seals and whales.

If you can, try and "Reduce, Reuse or **Recycle**" your toys. This will help the environment. If you do not want to play with a toy or game any more, you could do these things:

- Take it to a charity shop. Another child can then have it.
- Take it to a local play centre, nursery or pre-school.
- Put any plastic packaging in a recycling bin.

Ask an adult to help you.

1960s 1970s 1980s 1990s 2000s 2010s

Glossary

astronaut a person who travels into space

bonnet the front of a car

catapult a Y-shaped stick with elastic used to throw objects

clockwork something that can be wound up with a key to make it go

console panel with switches and buttons for controlling a device

cosmonaut an astronaut who comes from Russia

craze an activity or thing that is very popular with lots of people for a short time

electric something that uses electricity. Batteries used in toys make electricity.

environment the natural world of air, trees, plants, water and earth that we live in

gender whether you are male or female

handheld device electronic equipment that is small enough to be held in the hands

invent to think up and make something new

material a thing needed for an activity

miniature a model that is made to look just like an object but much smaller, such as a model car or train

recycle sort and collect rubbish so that it can be reused as something new

stuffed a toy with soft filling inside it

stuffing soft filling

technology the use of science to create new machines

weapon something used to injure or harm someone. A gun is a weapon.

World War I (1914–1918) war that took place between countries in many different parts of the world

Find out more

Books

Pastimes and Toys (Tell Me What You Remember), Sarah Ridley (Franklin Watts, 2019)

Ralph Baer: The Man Behind Video Games (Smithsonian Little Explorer: Little Inventor), Nancy Dickmann (Raintree, 2020)

The History of Computers (The History of Technology), Chris Oxlade (Raintree, 2017)

Toys (Start-up History), Jane Bingham & Ruth Nason (Franklin Watts, 2017)

Toys in the Past, Joanna Brundle (Booklife Publishing, 2017)

Websites

There are so many toys that it was not possible to include all of them in this book. You can find out more about toys and their history on these websites.

The Brighton Museums' website has a good short history of toys:
brightonmuseums.org.uk/discover/2012/05/21/toy-timeline/

Find out about what toys children played with in the 1800s, before the toys in this book were made:
www.dkfindout.com/uk/history/victorian-britain/childrens-games-and-toys/

Find out about the use of plastics in toy making:
www.dkfindout.com/uk/science/materials/plastics/

Index

action figures 18, 21, 25
ancient toys 4
Barbie dolls 15
board games 4, 10–11, 28
building sets 7, 9, 11, 18
catapult 6
clockwork toys 6, 8
computer games 11, 22, 24–25, 28
dolls 4, 6, 9, 15, 20, 23, 27, 28
electric toys 8, 9, 16, 19
electronic toys 16, 19, 20, 24
environment 29
eSports 26
Etch-a-Sketch 12
frisbees 12
handheld computer games 20, 22, 25
hula-hoops 12
Lego 18
loom bands 27
marbles 4
Meccano 7, 11
metal toys 5, 6, 7, 8–9, 11, 29
Mr Potato Head 12

outdoor games 6
"pet" toys 24, 27
plastic toys 5, 12–13, 18, 23, 29
Play-doh 14
puzzles 6
robots 19
Roosevelt, President Theodore "Teddy" 7
Rubik's Cube 23
space toys 19
space travel 19
Spirograph 18
Star Wars 20
teddy bears 7, 11, 28
toy inventors 5, 8, 15, 18, 21, 22
toy cars 5, 9, 13, 16, 18, 28
Toy of the Year Awards 18, 23
toy safety 10
train sets 8, 28
TV and film characters 17, 21, 25, 27
video game consoles 22, 25, 26
video games 11, 21, 22, 25, 26, 28
wartime toys 6, 11
wooden toys 4–5, 6, 18, 29
yo-yos 4